Dedicated to:
The children and families at
Caterpillar Cottage Preschool,
the medical professionals, first responders,
and essential service workers during the
2020 pandemic.

For information contact
Stuart Tartly Press 17216 Saticoy Street #226, Lake Balboa, CA 91406-2103

ISBN: 978-1-7337402-3-4

First Edition

Dear Parents,

The social-distancing we face in today's pandemic is unprecedented. All around the world, schools are closed and families are experiencing staying at home with their children, without playdates or park visits. And right now, we don't know how long this will last. Big feelings are natural reactions to this situation. It's hard for all of us; and parents are especially worried about how this might impact their little ones. Children's books are a wonderful medium to help children process new experiences.

Many of the parents in our preschool have voiced concerns about children's upsets about the changes in their daily lives. They miss going to school and they miss playing with friends. This book was initially written for them. Reading about emotions and concerns with children can help them gain context and validation for these confusing, and sometimes scary, feelings. Story times also provide children connected time with their adults where they might start to open up and talk more freely about their emotional experience.

We find that sometimes changing the words a bit to better fit the child's situation can make the story more personal and meaningful. You may already be doing this. An example might be to change Dad to Mom, Mommy or Grandma or Brother or Sister. Another helpful way to personalize it would be to pause and reflect, adding activities that your child has recently enjoyed with you.

I hope this is a helpful book for many.

Heather Malley

Not forever but for now,

I'm not going to my school,

or to the grocery store.

I'm staying home with my family.

I go on bug hunts in the backyard.

I make a picture to send to Grandma.

I talk to my friends and
teachers online.
But I want to be with them
in person.

I play with my mom, my dad or my sibling.

I play in my room.

I take a walk in my neighborhood
with my family. Sometimes we see our
neighbors wearing masks.

Not forever but for now,
I am staying home while the nurses and
doctors are taking care of some sick
people at the hospitals.

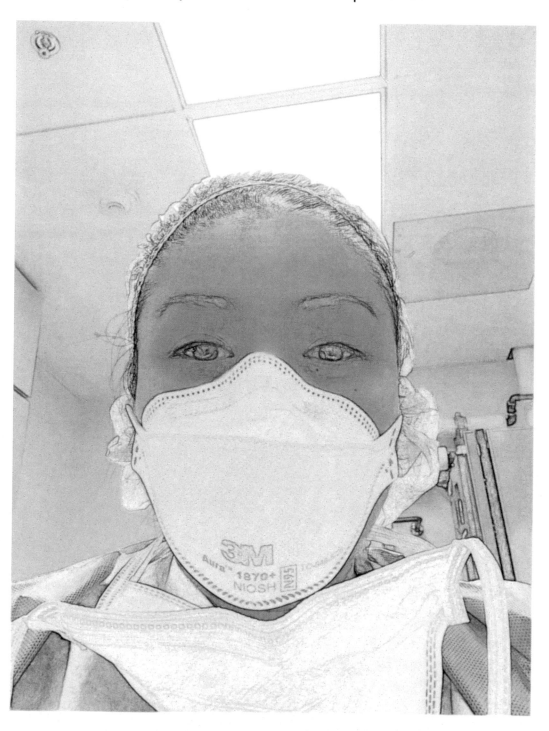

Sometimes I feel **sad**.
I sigh and sometimes cry.

I want to go somewhere with my
friends to play tag or pretend.
I want to go back to school.

I want to climb on the play structure at the
park, but there is caution tape there
telling us we can't.

Not forever but for now...

Sometimes I feel **mad**.
I stomp my feet. I yell!
I don't like that things are different.

I want the people to stop wearing the masks.
I want to see their faces.
I want to see children playing together again.

Some things are the same.

We have bedtime stories.

Sometimes I play a game with my parents and we laugh.

We make
muffins
together,
bring them
outside and
sit looking at
the clouds.

We wrestle and chase each other.
We snuggle.

Not forever but for now...

I want to know when I can play
with my friends again.

Sometimes I feel **scared** or **nervous**.
Sometimes I feel **shaky**.

I hug my mom

and hold my lovey.

And then my mom, or dad, holds me and says, "You are safe and loved and this is not forever, but it is for now."

Acknowledgements

This book would not be possible without the support of these lovely individuals:

My husband David, my parents, my daughter, My wonderful teachers and colleagues at our preschool Caterpillar Cottage (Andrea, Brenda, Adina), Susan North (mentor, friend and colleague), Mike Sherman, and the many parents children and friends of our preschool community who contributed their encouragement, input and photos for this project.